The Little Book of Bags, Boxes and Trays

Using Containers for Teaching and Learning

By Lynn

Illustrated by Kerry Ingham

Edited by Sally Featherstone

LITTLE BOOKS WITH BIG IDEAS

Published 2009 by A&C Black Publishers Limited
36 Soho Square, London W1D 3QY
www.acblack.com

First published by Featherstone Education, November 2004

ISBN 9781905019090

Text © Lynn Clere, 2004
Illustrations © Kerry Ingham, 2004
Series Editor, Sally Featherstone

A CIP record for this publication is available from the British Library.

Printed in Great Britain by Latimer Trend & Company Limited.

This book is produced using paper that is made from wood grown in
managed, sustainable forests. It is natural, renewable and recyclable.

The logging and manufacturing processes conform to the environmental
regulations of the country of origin.

**To see our full range of titles
visit www.acblack.com**

Contents

Introduction

Children learn most effectively when they are actively doing, making, singing and exploring. The 'wow' factor becomes evident when the activity requires the children to use all of their senses, to use their whole bodies, and to stay active.

Resources should be varied – they should include natural materials and resources that have been made, bought or collected to satisfy the specific learning intentions for the activity. Learning is particularly effective if the children have been able to help with collecting or making of the materials.

Themed bags and boxes
contain objects or resources which form a collection. These can be:

▶ linked to a specific activity or set of learning intentions;

▶ collections of similar items;

▶ resources to support role play;

▶ props for a specific story;

▶ collections to develop particular skills and competencies;

▶ resources for a game;

▶ surprises and challenges to enjoy, to puzzle over and to think about.

Keeping the objects together in one bag or box serves two purposes.

▶ Children love the surprise element of what is in the container. They also enjoy emptying and refilling the bag or box.

▶ The bag or box provides an immediate tidying up and storage facility, ensuring that when the learning focus changes, the resources will not be lost, and will be available when the topic/story/activity is revisited. This way of working also helps if your setting is in a shared building.

Bags and boxes will not remain static or finished. They will almost certainly evolve as children add to the collection or ask if they can make a collection of their own.

Settling in and Special Needs
If a child finds settling in difficult, or if they have Special Educational Needs, they may enjoy having their own interest box – a collection of objects personal to them, which helps them feel secure and valued. Involve parents when making these collections!

Some children may want to continue playing with resources that have been replaced by a new topic, or if they have enjoyed the role play area which is now going to be changed. In these cases, boxes can be stored with your open access resources, so that the children can continue to enjoy them.

Types of bags and boxes

Storysacks

These contain a range of items to support a particular story book. These may include a toy character from the book, an audio tape of the story or related songs, or a non-fiction book related to the story.

Story boxes

These can be made from any boxes. The box contains the resources to re-enact a favourite story, nursery or counting rhyme. Related toys, puppets and artefacts are included so that children can act out the nursery rhyme, counting rhyme, story, or play scenario.

Heuristic play bags

These contain items which should be used purely for exploratory play. They contain quantities of objects such as corks, cones, beads, tops, lids, pegs (with an emphasis on natural materials, textures and colours – wood, metal, cork). Their use is specific and focuses on child-initiated, exploratory play, encouraging skills such as hand/eye co-ordination, observation and exploration.

The use of Heuristic Play is explored further in 'People Under Three' by Eleanor Goldschmeid.

Treasure baskets and Investigation boxes

Similar in some respects to heuristic play bags, these collections provide exploratory play opportunities, and can be themed, for example, a magnets box, a scents basket, a fine manipulative skills box etc.

For more ideas see 'The Little Book of Treasure Baskets' published by Featherstone.

What's in the box?

This is usually included as a Circle Time activity. A small box can be passed around the circle, and children guess what might be inside the box. When the box has been felt, shaken and otherwise explored, and each child has had a guess, the box can then be opened. The item is passed around for the children to explore, and they can guess who it may belong to, why they have left it here, what is it used for etc.

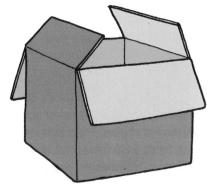

Themed activity bags

These are collections which usually focus on a story, rhyme or relate to a particular learning intention within the Early Learning Goals such as pattern, time or initial letter recognition.

Scenario trays

Shallow washing up bowls or cat litter trays can be used as scenario trays for small world play, as in the Going On a Bear Hunt trays (see pages 46 and 47). Children become part of the story as they role play what happened.

A box doesn't have to be a cuboid!

Cylindrical tubes can offer lots of play and learning opportunities e.g. a large tube filled with cars which can be opened to make a road tunnel etc.

And it doesn't have to be in a box!

If a container is being used as one of the props, then you can use this to store the rest of the resources:

▶ a decorator's bucket containing a variety of decorating resources can also be used to hold paint or water (see The Painter's Box, pages 42 and 43).

▶ a builder's or gardener's wheelbarrow (see Gardener's Barrow, pages 32 and can 33) be filled with the tools of the trade!

▶ Mr Gumpy's boat can be a big container (even a small plastic boat) containing blue fabric for the river, character bibs, the story, and a picnic (see Mr Gumpy's Outing, pages 52 and 53). The expense of the plastic play boat could be justified by also using it as an outdoor sand or water tray.

Interest boxes and Inclusion

An interest box is a collection of objects that:

▶ appeals to a particular group of children (e.g. shared interest in animals or the farm);
▶ supports the current curriculum topic (e.g. bucket filled with items from the seaside);
▶ focuses on one type of object (e.g. basket of objects made of wood);
▶ have special significance for a child with Special educational Needs.

Boxes and basket for children who have Special Educational Needs are usually intended to encourage language development, develop concentration skills or support personal and social development. Children are more likely to engage with resources that interest them, and interest baskets are particularly helpful for children whose difficulties lie on the Autistic Spectrum.

Links with the Early Learning Goals

Themed bags and boxes are a holistic method of teaching and learning, and each bag will contribute to several of the areas of learning within the Foundation Stage Guidance.

The activities within this book will enable children to work towards the following Early Learning Goals:

▶ Work as part of a group or class, taking turns and sharing fairly. **PSED**

▶ Select and use activities and resources independently. **PSED**

▶ Extend their vocabulary, exploring meanings and sounds of new words. **CLL**

▶ Use language to imagine and recreate roles and experiences. **CLL**

▶ Know that print carries meaning. **CLL**

▶ Attempt writing for different purposes. **CLL**

▶ Say and use number names in order in familiar contexts. **MD**

▶ Count reliably up to 10 everyday objects. **MD**

▶ Recognise numerals 1–9. **MD**

▶ Talk about, recognise and recreate simple patterns. **MD**

▶ Investigate objects and materials by using all of their senses as appropriate. **KUW**

▶ Select the tools and techniques they need to shape, assemble and join materials they are using. **KUW**

▶ Find out about past and present events in their own lives. **KUW**

▶ Find out about their environment and talk about those features they like and dislike. **KUW**

▶ Use a range of small and large equipment. **PD**

▶ Handle tools, objects, construction and malleable materials safely and with increasing control. **PD**

▶ Explore colour, texture, shape, form and space in 2 or 3 dimensions. **CD**

▶ Respond in a variety of ways to what they see, hear, smell, touch, feel. **CD**

Experience of working with themed bags and boxes helps towards one of the most important of the Early Learning Goals:

'Continue to be interested, excited and motivated to learn.' **PSED**

The Finger Box

Focus: **for fine motor skills**

The container: a large plastic crate

What you need

▶ a mat to tip the contents out on to

and some of the following:

▶ light switches
▶ a kaleidoscope
▶ pipe cleaners
▶ traditional and pincer grip castanets
▶ plastic screw-topped jars
▶ small boxes with lids
▶ paper clips and bull dog clips
▶ clothes pegs
▶ tubs of dough and plastic plates
▶ rubbers, pencil sharpeners, pencils
▶ pens with click down ends
▶ pens that change colour on each click
▶ glitter glue pens
▶ glue sticks
▶ brass fold down clips
▶ paper crimpers

▶ staplers and staples
▶ hole punches
▶ pattern and picture punches
▶ beads and threading string
▶ ribbons and weaving frames
▶ peel off stickers
▶ Blu-tack and Sellotape
▶ play dough and air dry modelling clay
▶ beads, plastic tweezers, droppers, chopsticks
▶ pattern and traditional scissors
▶ a variety of paper and card

I will need

This box encourages fine motor skills and promotes the finger strength and dexterity needed for early writing skills to develop.
Children enjoy seeing all the activities put out together and sorting through them.

What you do

1. Sit with the children and help them choose some of the activities, showing them how the resources work and what you can do with them. Encourage them to have a go, and allow time for the children to work at their own pace. Once the children know about this box, the activity could be offered for free access, as it will become a popular activity, which children will return to again and again.

2. Place smaller items i.e. paper clips, beads, staples etc in screw-topped jars and lidded boxes and tubs, as just opening these will support fine manipulative skills.

Further activities and curriculum links:

▶ Put the box near the writing table, as many activities would support the writing table activities.

▶ Use the materials to make simple projects - e.g. collage boards, showing how different materials can be changed using crimping machines (PD, KUW)

▶ Making cards for friends and family (CLL)

▶ Use the pipe cleaners, card, dough etc. to make simple puppets (PD,CD)

▶ Count or sort small beads into egg cartons or small pots, using the chopsticks or tweezers (PD, MD)

And another idea...

▶ Use the box in the creative area. It will encourage children to make their own card designs at Christmas, Mothers' Day etc. Their card designs will be unique and individual, not adult directed. This encourages real creativity.

Some Key Words

▶ hold	▶ tweeze
▶ turn	▶ sort
▶ pull	▶ choose
▶ twist	▶ small
▶ grip	▶ fingers

The Feelings Bag

Focus: **a bag for thinking**

The container: a drawstring bag

What you need

- drawstring fabric bag (ideally with faces printed or drawn on it)
- emotions masks
- laminated 'How do you feel today?' chart and dry wipe pen
- dice with a different emotion picture on each face
- smiley stickers
- books about feelings
- emotions faces, stamps and pads
- happy and sad finger puppets
- a 'worry' bear or doll to share worries with
- pens and paper
- a familiar puppet as a focus for stories and situations
- child safe mirrors
- disposable/digital camera

A useful bag for introducing PSED activities into morning registration, whether this is done by an adult or the children register themselves. Asking how a child feels will tell you what sort of day to expect - forewarned is forearmed!

What you do

1. Introduce the concept and explore the contents of the bag. Which is the happy mask? How do we know? What emotions do the other masks show? Look at the books.

2. Explain that you can tell the Worry Bear anything that makes you happy or sad, excited or frightened. Invite the children to think of a name for the bear.

3. Talk to the children about how they feel. What do they like doing at nursery/school. What makes them happy and what makes them sad? How do we look when we are happy/sad?

4. Make happy/sad/cross/tired faces at each other. Look in the mirror at all the different faces you can make.

Further activities and curriculum links:

▶ Keep a daily chart of how we feel. The children fill this by drawing smiley/sad faces or putting stickers by their name. This can be a valuable activity for children with Special Educational needs or who may be experiencing difficulties at home or at school. (PSED)

▶ Keep the emotions sack readily available. The children can then access the bag independently and share with each other how they are feeling. (PSED)

And another idea...

▶ Find an alliterative name for your worry bear – William or Wilma Worry bear or a Caring bear – Cara or Kieran.

▶ Make alliterative names for the children: Jumping Jack, Laughing Lisa. Children love this game!

Some Key Words

▶ happy	▶ scared
▶ sad	▶ excited
▶ worried	▶ lonely
▶ angry	▶ feelings
▶ sorry	

The Friendship Box

Focus: **make a new friend**

The container: **a plastic craft box**

What you need

- a plastic craft box with compartments, or a carry work box with lift out trays
- beads – different colours and sizes,
- novelty beads: i.e. cars, trucks, animals, letters, stars, fruit, etc.
- novelty buttons
- embroidery thread, thin ribbon, braid, laces, round elastic

- a long length (10m) of ribbon or braid
- books and stories about friends
- a copy of the story of the Hindu god Indra

This box can help to unite individuals into a group. Making a friendship bracelet for a friend can help to build relationships, especially in a new class or group. The activity can also be linked to the Hindu festival of Raksha Bandhan, when brothers and sisters make bracelets for each other.

What you do

1. Read or tell a story about friends, friendship and working together.

2. Talk about friendship and how important it is for us to get along with each other and to work together. Ask them who their friends are in the class, and what a good friend does and says.

3. As part of a circle/PSED activity encourage the children to talk or play with someone they would not normally talk to or play with.

4. Watch for 'good friends' and talk about what they do, using real examples of children from your setting. Be clear about what they did and said, how they helped another child, worked together, said something kind, helped someone lonely or sad.

Further activities and curriculum links:

▶ Use a long length of braid or ribbon to make a 'friendship web'. The children sit in a circle. One child holds the end of the ribbon and passes it through their hands to a friend in the circle, saying something positive about their friend as they do so. As the activity continues, a web is created which can be reused or displayed. (PSED, PD)

▶ Make friendship bracelets linked to the Hindu festival of Raksha Bandhan – a Hindu festival when girls tie silk or cotton bracelets around their brothers' wrists to protect them from danger. (KUW)

And another idea...

▶ Invite a Hindu to come into your setting to talk about their culture.

▶ Invite two adult friends to talk to the children about what being a being a good friend means to them.

Some Key Words	
▶ friends	▶ braid
▶ sharing	▶ beads
▶ web	▶ play
▶ kind	▶ care
▶ ribbon	▶ together

The Weather Box

Focus: **a box for outside**

The container: a large plastic crate with a lid

What you need

- a large plastic crate with lid
- laminated weather chart and symbols
- windmills, wind sock, wind chimes
- kites
- deep plastic trays
- spray bottles, water and food colour
- window scrapers
- vegetable or baby oil and pipettes
- washing up liquid
- children's umbrellas
- chalk
- a battery operated tape recorder
- weather songs CD, tape and blank tapes
- suitable outdoor thermometer
- plastic bottles for rain gauges

Young children should be able to play outdoors regardless of the weather. Invest in some waterproof clothing, or ask parents to ensure that their children are suitably dressed. If children are warm and protected from the wet they will enjoy playing outside in all weathers.

What you do

1. Begin an interest in the weather by talking about it each morning. Discuss what the weather was like on the way from home.

2. Make a weather chart together, and show the children how to fill it in as part of registration or group time.

3. Show the children that you enjoy being outside! Draw their attention to the changing weather and seasons. Point out and discuss features of the weather in your garden or outside area - the wind blowing the leaves on the ground, clouds racing, raindrops on the windows, frost in a shady corner, the moving shadows in summer, an evaporating puddle, etc.

Further activities and curriculum links:

▶ During appropriate weather, show the children how to use resources from the box. When it is sunny, draw round their shadows with the chalk, collect rainwater, hang wind chimes or wind socks on a windy day. Add food dye, washing up liquid or oil to puddles or snow and watch what happens. (KUW)

▶ Collect rain snow, hail or ice in a tray and bring it indoors so you can watch as it melts, and discuss why this happens. (KUW)

▶ Record an account of each day's weather on an audio tape. (CLL, KUW)

And another idea...

▶ Make your own kites on a windy day using black bin bag plastic or carrier bags and string. Take them outside to fly.

▶ Show a video of TV weather. Set up the role play area as the weather studio with a map of the UK and velcro backed weather symbols.

Some Key Words

▶ weather	▶ cold	
▶ raining	▶ snow	
▶ sunny	▶ dry	
▶ windy	▶ wet	
▶ hot	▶ cloudy	
▶ foggy	▶ thunder	
▶ misty		

Writing Boxes

The container: **plastic lunch boxes**

What you need

- lunch boxes with carry handles
- dry wipe pens and white boards
- pens, pencils, scissors, tape
- highlighter pen and laminated text
- note and memo pads
- telephone/address books, diaries
- stationery - christening, birthday invitations, notelets, cards
- envelopes, coloured paper, card
- paper with clip art or borders
- Post-it pads (and a board in the room to display them)
- staplers and hole punches
- blank card to make your own card
- paper of all sorts, sizes, shapes, colours, squared paper, lined paper, tissue, tracing
- stickers, stamps and pads

These boxes are popular, so you will probably need to make several of them. Easily transported to different activities indoors and outside, they are always in use! The containers are children's lunch boxes. The drinks flask inside the box is used to hold felt tips, pens, scissors, pencils etc.

What you do

1. Introduce the writing boxes, and show the contents of the different boxes. (Put different things in each box to maintain interest or change the contents regularly.)

2. Talk about the sorts of writing we do - shopping lists, to-do lists, letters, birthday cards, reminders, diaries, messages, etc.

3. Let the children see you writing during the day, and when you are writing encourage them look at what you are writing and how you write.
    Talk about what you are doing and how writing works. Say helpful things, like 'I'm starting at the top. Now I'm going to write a note to Mrs... It says ....' or 'I need to remind myself to buy.... for tea.'

Further activities and curriculum links:

▶ Encourage the children to take the cases with them indoors and outside – drawing a picture of the model they have made, writing a birthday card, making a list, recording scores in a game.

▶ Set up an indoor and an outdoor message board where the children can leave messages for each other, for the group and for you. Leave messages yourself for the children. (CL,PD)

▶ Give each child their own jotter pad for a drawing/writing diary. (PD,CLL)

And another idea...

▶ Liaise with colleagues at other settings and organise a letter exchange.
▶ Send each other whole class letters either by post or e-mail.
▶ Encourage children to make labels, signs and notices.

Some Key Words
▶ writing
▶ pen
▶ paper
▶ message
▶ letter
▶ send
▶ post
▶ invite
▶ label
▶ list

Maths Story Boxes

Focus: **fun with counting and sorting**

The container: a variety of boxes and containers

What you need for:

A picnic box

- ▶ a picnic hamper
- ▶ a picnic blanket
- ▶ 4 sets of coloured plastic plates, cups, forks, knives, spoons
- ▶ some plastic or dough food
  Use for matching and one to one.

What you need for:

A teddies picnic

- ▶ a large birthday gift bag
- ▶ 4 or 5 different sized teddies
- ▶ 3–5 play dough birthday cakes with candles from 1–3 or 1–5.
- ▶ 3 or 5 Birthday cards with '1 Today,' '2 Today' etc.
- ▶ velcro badges : 'I am 1, 2, 3...' and hats with spots or numbers.
  Use for sequencing and counting.

Maths story boxes are easy to make. They are lots of fun and packed with practical maths opportunities. In these activities children are counting, matching one to one, and recognising numbers for a purpose. The boxes also develop PSED skills by encouraging children to work together.

What you need for:

Parking your car

- ▶ divide a toy garage into parking spaces with strips of masking tape. Number the spaces with dots or numbers.
- ▶ number the cars with numerals 1, 2, 3, etc. The children must park their cars in the correct space.

Use for matching, extending the number of cars as children learn new numbers.

Extend into ordinal numbers (first, second, third).

What you need for:

Supermarket dash!

- ▶ a child's shopping trolley
- ▶ a whiteboard shopping list and pens
- ▶ toy food items or empty packing
- ▶ a bag to take your shopping home
- ▶ money and purse, till
- ▶ a sand timer

Set up the supermarket shelves (on a table or the carpet). Give the children a shopping list. They must find the items on the list and tick them off as they go. Lists can be pictures or words. Time how quickly they can get all the items correctly.

Colour and Pattern Bags

Focus: **bags of patterns**

The container: **fabric bags**

What you need

Three bags made from fake fur, animal prints or other prints with bold patterns.

Bag 1:

▶ 2 sets of laminated clip art cards of animals with different fur or skin patterns

▶ fabrics with patterns and prints, big enough to dress up in

Bag 2:

▶ Small fabric samples with different patterns – spots, stripes, checks

▶ Post-it notes, a pack of felt-tip pens

Bag 3:

▶ pictures of girls and boys with different patterned clothes

▶ blank card templates of the above

▶ felt-tip pens

Awareness of pattern is a key concept running through early mathematics. These bags introduce the concept of pattern, which children need to be aware of before they can reach the Early Learning Goal 'Talk about, recognise and recreate simple patterns'.

What you do

1. **Use Bag 1** for sorting and matching the two animals with the same patterns e.g. two zebras, two leopards. Use the cards to play pairs and snap.

2. **Use Bag 2** to explore patterns, by looking at the fabric swatches talking about the pattern on each. Then everyone can draw their favourite or create their own pattern on a Post-it note. The Post-its can then be displayed together as a patchwork pattern quilt.

3. **Use Bag 3** for sorting into sets – those wearing stripes/dots etc. The children can then make new sets with different patterns, using the templates. Display these different patterns as sets of children in the same 'family'.

Further activities and curriculum links:

▶ Make a big patchwork pattern with squares of different fabrics. Cut a black bin bag open, tape it to a table or the floor and offer the children a big bag of mixed fabric squares. They can take the squares out one at a time and stick them on the plastic with very dilute PVA glue. Finish by painting the whole quilt with dilute glue and leave to dry. Peel the plastic off to get a big patchwork picture. (MD, CLL, CD, PSED)

And another idea...

▶ Make your own themed wallpaper for the role play area. Use lining paper, paint and themed stamps - car and lorry stamps for a garage area; bear stamps for the Three Bears' House; flowers for a garden centre.

Some Key Words
▶ pattern
▶ colour names
▶ spots
▶ dots
▶ lines
▶ stripes
▶ checks
▶ tartan
▶ wiggles
▶ waves

Maths Games Rucksack

Focus: maths outside

What you need

- a large rucksack
- jacks or fivestones game
- skipping rope, bats, balls, marbles
- balls – from football size to small bouncy balls, bat and ball games, catching and throwing games
- laminated playing cards
- laminated dominoes
- playground chalks for hopscotch
- number bean bags
- laminated tally score cards or whiteboards and dry wipe pens
- a score notebook and pen
- a large floor dice

This rucksack can be easily transported by the children. Keep it on a hook near the door, where they can see it as they go out, and help themselves to it. The contents will encourage them to keep a tally of their scores in games, use number for a purpose and continue to play traditional games.

What you do

1. Look through the rucksack with the children.
2. Talk about all the different games you could play with the equipment, and discuss the rules. Play a short game with them, then leave the children to play traditional or made-up games.
3. At the end of each session, get the children to share the games they have played, with demonstrations if possible.

Further activities and curriculum links:

▶ Have a carousel of the above games so teams of children can compete in a playground 'Olympic Games'! (PSED, PD)

▶ Use the chalk to make: Hopscotch Games (CLL, CD)
Number stepping stones for jumping games. Number counting ladders and number lines for counting games using bean bags and big dice. Add card and bigger pens to the bag for numbering vehicles or parking places

▶ Hang blackboards or whiteboards on fences and walls, so children can score games and write numbers or notices (MD, CLL)

And another idea...

▶ Take the bag out for group games sessions where you play maths games or sing number songs.

▶ Add a book of playground games to the rucksack and learn some new ones with the children.

Some Key Words
▶ throw
▶ catch
▶ ball
▶ goal
▶ score
▶ tally
▶ colour
▶ team
▶ number
▶ win

An Explorer's Rucksack

Focus: inspire an adventure

> The container: **a rucksack**

What you need

- a rucksack
- magnifying glasses
- children's microscopic viewer
- child-proof outdoor thermometer
- small books on spotting wildlife
- magnet, torch
- compass
- notebook and pen
- disposable camera
- sandwich box and water bottle
- binoculars
- map

Children love to explore their environment. Even in a city, a Foundation Stage garden is full of wildlife, surprises and new things. This rucksack will encourage children to search for and nurture the wildlife around them. The children will love setting out on their very own expedition of discovery!

What you do

1. Let the children help you to put the rucksack together.
2. Can they name all of the items? Show them (or get the children to demonstrate) how to use each item.
3. Look through nature books and talk about what they might find in the garden - the types of flowers and trees, the different shapes of the leaves.
4. Look at pictures of spiders, snails, slugs and worms. Some children may be genuinely afraid of such creatures, others will have acquired their prejudice from others. Talk about proper care and handling of any creatures they find.

Further activities and curriculum links:

▶ Give opportunities for children to draw or take photographs of what they see when they go out exploring. (KUW, PD, CD)

▶ Help them to find out more about what they have found. Can you help them to do simple research in books or on a CD-ROM? (KUW, CLL)

▶ Use the viewers to look at plants and insects and to show these to others. (PSED, KUW)

▶ Discuss how minibeasts must be returned to their original habitat, and make sure that the children do so. (CLL, KUW, PSED)

And another idea...

▶ Use a tall, transparent plastic sweet jar to make a wormery. Add some compost and some garden worms. The children will be able to see how the worms make tunnels within the compost.
Get wormery kits from Insect Lore.

Some Key Words	
▶ magnify	▶ careful
▶ hot	▶ ladybird
▶ cold	▶ worm
▶ compass	▶ slug
▶ worm	▶ snail
▶ viewer	

Outdoor Weaving Box

Focus: more fine motor fun!

The container: a large plastic crate with a lid

What you need

- a large crate with a lid so that you can store the materials outside if possible
- coloured ribbon in different widths (floristry ribbon is good as it weathers well outside – ask your local shop)
- wool and string
- pliable plant material, such as living willow
- feathers
- flowers (garden or silk)
- twigs, leaves, beads
- gift ribbon, foil, cellophane
- builders' netting (available from builders' merchants)
- large pieces of netting, trellis
- hessian or other material which has an open weave texture

I will need

This is a good outdoor activity, as you can weave on large areas. It is colourful and the end results will enhance your garden. Some settings have chain fencing which can look a little bleak, but is transformed by the children's weaving. Adding 'found objects' will give another dimension.

What you do

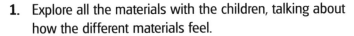

1. Explore all the materials with the children, talking about how the different materials feel.

2. Tie a piece of netting or trellis to the fence or hooks in door frames or walls. You could hang hessian or netting from a washing line or a long cane.

3. Work alongside the children to weave the different materials in and out. Tie objects on the weaving or thread them on the ribbon as you weave. Decorate the hanging with feathers, shells, leaves, stones, beads and flowers.

Further activities and curriculum links:

▶ With the children weave numbers 0–10 in ribbon in the fence. Tie off the ends to make a permanent number line. Number the cars and bike so that the children can park them tidily along the number line. (MD, PD, PSED – see 'A Place to Learn', produced by Lewisham LEA).

▶ Go on a walk in the park or the country and collect things to add to your weavings. You could make an Autumn hanging with seeds, leaves, twigs and flowers. (CLL, PD, CD)

And another idea...

▶ Give children a bag of their own to collect things on a walk. Then use hessian and big needles to make individual hangings or mats.

▶ Make a weaving frame from wood and try weaving across strings.

Some Key Words

▶	weave	▶	in and out
▶	ribbon	▶	up/down
▶	netting	▶	tie
▶	trellis	▶	string
▶	fence	▶	fingers

Natural Arts Box

The container: a large plastic or card box

What you need

- a large, plain papier maché or cardboard box with a lid. If possible get one with compartments and drawers
- shells
- unusually marked pebbles
- feathers
- cones (open and closed)
- conkers, acorns, nuts
- Sycamore and other winged fruits

- leaves from different trees (pick up more in autumn for their colour)
- sprigs of spring blossom
- twigs and stems
- dried grasses and seed heads
- herb leaves and stems of rosemary, lavender, mint. Ears of wheat, barley or oats
- bark, ferns, skeleton leaves

N.B. Be aware of allergies and poisonous plants, leaves, berries and fruit.

This box encourages children to be aware of natural resources around them, and can help to cultivate a recycling culture. Playing with natural products and colours is known to be calming and creative and appeals to all the senses by including scented, textured and sound making items.

What you do

1. Take photographs of patterns and prints in your garden or setting: registration plates of staff cars, reception notices, the setting name, the pattern of fencing, trellis and tree bark in the garden, game markings on the playground, the wooden boards on the toy shed door, brick patterns in walls and paths, edges of paths and flower beds.

2. Show the pictures to the children and see if they can tell you what they are and where they are. Go out in small groups to match the photos to the real objects. If you are going to let the children use this bag independently, limit the photos to safe places!

3. Let the children use the camera to record new patterns and marks they see. Raindrops on windows, patterns on socks, snail trails on walls.

Further activities and curriculum links:

▶ Try recreating the patterns you all find. Make wax crayon rubbings of the bark texture or bricks; use clipboards or whiteboards to copy patterns outside. (PD, CD, MD, KUW)

▶ Use the photos to make new number plates for the bikes and trikes. (PSED, MD, CLL)

▶ Arrange lolly sticks in the patterns of fencing. (PD, MD, KUW)

▶ Build Lego bricks in the patterns you see in walls and paths. (PD, MD, KUW)

And another idea...

▶ Go on a pattern and print trail in your local area. Look for road and shop signs, road markings, traffic lights, bus stops, notices. Take photos.

▶ Make a scrapbook of patterns and signs. Add samples of fabrics with different patterns and textures.

Some Key Words

▶ pattern   ▶ corner
▶ zig zag   ▶ shop
▶ lights   ▶ street
▶ camera   ▶ lines
▶ crossing   ▶ notice
▶ sign   ▶ writing

Collect a Sound

Focus: initial letters with a difference

The container: **a set of drawers or shoe boxes**

What you need

▶ a chest with several drawers

▶ a vinyl, plastic or card letter for each letter of the alphabet

▶ initial letter books

▶ artefacts for your chosen letters

▶ some small baskets for children to collect and sort artefacts

▶ an alphabet mat

▶ a letter sounds audio tape

▶ small laminated name cards for each child

▶ small laminated photographs of each child in the group

Search for some small sets of drawers or make your own for this new version of initial sound collection. You could use plywood drawers from craft shops or plastic drawers from DIY stores. Younger children could use shoe boxes with the ends cut to make a little door.

What you do

1. Stick a letter of the alphabet on each drawer of your set. Start with just one or two drawers and add more as children learn to recognise each sound and letter. In Reception, you could continue until you have a complete set from A-Z. Make sure the drawers are big enough to put things in, and 'plant' some smaller items around the room to ensure success in finding more!

2. Talk about the sound drawers with the children and explain what you are doing. Let them help you to put a book about that letter, and an item which has that initial sound in each drawer. With younger children, stick an item on the outside of the drawer or door too.

3. Let them trace with their finger over the letter, so they become familiar with its shape and how it is written.

4. Now suggest that the children could collect items from home or in your setting to put in the drawers.

Further activities and curriculum links:

▶ Offer a basket of small items with different initial letter sounds and ask the children to put them in the correct drawer. (CLL, MD)

▶ Tip out the contents of two (or more) drawers and challenge the children to put them back in the right drawer. (CLL)

And another idea...

▶ Use the name cards or photos for a 'sorting by sound' game.

▶ Tip out some drawers and put the contents on the right sounds on an alphabet mat; or use the drawer idea for numbers 1–10.

Some Key Words	
▶ drawer	▶ find
▶ sort	▶ sound
▶ put	▶ listen
▶ list	▶ same
▶ collect	▶ different

Rhyme Time

Focus: stories for counting

The container: cat litter trays

What you need for:

Five Green Bottles

▶ a tray covered in brick paper
▶ five empty green plastic water bottles labelled 1–5
▶ a laminated copy of the rhyme with picture prompts

Turn the tray upside down to play the game as you sing the song. Use the tray for free play, and sometimes play it out of doors.

What you need for:

Humpty Dumpty

▶ a wall box as for the five Green Bottles box
▶ finger puppets of Humpty Dumpty the king and his men which can be brought out to play and then stored away inside the box.
▶ a laminated copy of the rhyme with picture prompts

Use the tray on its side or upside down as you play and sing the song.

Number and counting is much easier when you use nursery and counting rhymes. The boxes here are (unused!) cat litter trays. Cheap and colourful, they are deep enough to hold a range of resources and can be stacked away on a shelf when not in use. They are also light and easily carried.

What you need for:

Five Currant Buns

- ▶ a tray (you could make hole and thread a string through so it can hang round a child's neck)
- ▶ five buns made from dough
- ▶ plastic pennies in a purse
- ▶ a headband for the baker and five more for children shopping
- ▶ a laminated copy of the rhyme with picture prompts

What you need for:

Five Little Monkeys

- ▶ a brown tray
- ▶ a box covered in fabric for a bed
- ▶ finger puppets or small world people for the doctor and mother
- ▶ monkey figures or puppets numbered 1–5
- ▶ a laminated copy of the rhyme with picture prompts

Use the tray for group or independent play.

What you need for:

Five Fat Sausages

- ▶ a large frying pan
- ▶ five plastic sausages (from the home corner or dogs' toys. These squeaky sausages with faces from pet shops are lots more fun)
- ▶ two percussion instruments for the 'pop' and 'bang'
- ▶ a laminated copy of the rhyme with picture prompts. Children love this noisy game!

What you need for:

Incy Wincy Spider

- ▶ a tray on its side
- ▶ a kitchen roll tube for the drain
- ▶ a big plastic spider on elastic
- ▶ sun and rain pictures on lolly sticks
- ▶ a laminated copy of the rhyme with picture prompts.

Move the spider down inside and out of the tube following the words of the song. Plastic spiders (even big ones) are safely scary!

What you need for:

Five Little Speckled Frogs

- ▶ a green tray
- ▶ blue fabric or plastic for the pond (or a dish for water!)
- ▶ a wooden log
- ▶ 5 plastic frogs (with spots or 1–5 number stickers on their backs)
- ▶ a laminated copy of the rhyme with picture prompts

I Remember When and Where

Focus: **time and place**

The container: boxes with lids

What you need for:

Do You Remember?

▶ a lidded box (a shoe box is fine)

▶ photographs of children and staff taken within the setting over the year, to record events, visits, visitors etc.

Look at the photos and talk about your shared memories of the term or year.

Look at your setting in different seasons and at different times of the day.

What you need for:

When I was a Baby

▶ a lidded box

▶ photographs of children and staff when they were babies and when they were younger

Guess who the babies are. Sort the photos into a time line of youngest to oldest. Look at different clothes, toys, hairstyles, etc.

Time is a difficult concept to teach, and these boxes may help. Children need to understand the passing of time; past, present and future, night and day, and sequences of events. They need wide experience of the passing of time before they can begin to understand and read clocks.

What you need for

Tell me the time

- a larger box, again covered in an appropriate paper
- old watches (wrist, fob and nurse's), clocks, alarm, digital and analogue
- egg timers; a simple stopwatch
- cooking timer
- rain machines
- photo album with pictures of clocks in public places and on household appliances – microwaves, video machine, TV
- a pictorial timetable for your setting – what happens when
- television magazine; a timetable for the local bus and train
- calendars and diaries
- story and reference books about time
- card clocks with moveable hands

1. Show the children all the resources and give them plenty of time to play freely with the items and to ask questions.
2. Show them how you can time activities such as tidy up time or have races with egg timers or stop watches.
3. Show the children the alarm clock and cooking timer and talk about what they are used for at home. Set an alarm clock or cooking timer for outside time or tidy up time.
4. Look at calendars and diaries, and make your own versions to plan and record events in your setting.
5. Make references to clocks and watches as you work. Sometimes say 'In five minutes,' or 'When the big hand gets to... it's time for snack.'

What you need for:

A Christmas/Birthday Box

- a lidded box covered with Christmas/birthday paper.
- Christmas decorations, cards, stockings, stories, presents or
- birthday cards, candles, badges, stories, photos, etc. with picture prompts.

   Give plenty of time for free play with the contents and sharing memories before a more structured discussion.

The Painter's box

Focus: a bucket full of fun

The container: a big decorator's bucket

What you need

- a variety of different sized paint brushes
- small rollers and trays
- bottles of ready mixed paint in primary colours, mixing pots
- tub of sand to make texture paint
- stamps to make wallpaper designs
- bottle of water for water painting
- car windscreen scraper
- a tape measure

- a spirit level
- plumb line and chalk line
- roll of lining paper
- overalls, aprons, goggles, masks
- customer list, diary, notepad, pens
- 'Wet Paint' signs, dust sheets
- paint colour charts
- mobile phone
- DIY magazines

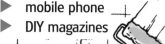

This box is easy for children to carry around as they play, and the contents can all be bought from DIY shops. The bucket can also be used to hold water or paint. You could cover the outside with pictures and photos of tools from magazines and catalogues.

What you do

1. Discuss with the children about what decorators do and how they work. Find out what they already know. Collect a list of words they need or use (to add to the ones in the Key Words box).

2. Talk to the children about the things they think a decorator needs. If possible, go shopping together to get them. Look at magazines, books and maybe record some home makeover programmes for them to watch.

3. When you have collected all the contents of the bucket together, let the children play freely with it first, before introducing some more structured activities to extend their play.

Further activities and curriculum links:

▶ Writing customer quotes, diary entries, print awareness, phoning customers, taking messages (signs). (CLL)

▶ Finding ways to measuring areas to be decorated. (MA)

▶ Making their own wallpaper, recognising and creating patterns. (MA)

▶ Number recognition; sequencing. (MA).

▶ Changing materials, colour mixing and making textured paint. (MA)

▶ Using a range of painting equipment, role play. (CR)

▶ Sharing, taking turns and working together. (PSED)

And another idea...

▶ Get a decorator to visit, or use a time when redecoration is happening in your setting, for children to see decorators in action.

▶ Redecorate your home corner – paint the furniture, paper the walls.

Some Key Words

▶ paper
▶ paint
▶ brush
▶ decorate
▶ cost
▶ measure
▶ colour
▶ new
▶ favourite
▶ different

Whatever Next!

Focus: a story box for a favourite story

The container: a large cardboard box

What you need

- a cardboard box – large enough for the children to get inside
- 'FRAGILE' stickers
- a pair of wellington boots
- a large colander
- a teddy bear
- food for the journey
- a copy of the story 'Whatever Next!' (published by Macmillan Children's books)

Acting out a story helps children to understand and remember it, and bags or boxes which help them to do this are always popular. Imagination and creativity are at the heart of story telling, and children will use the box or bag time after time to revisit and revise the story.

What you do

1. Read the story with the children.
2. Talk about the Little Bear's journey and the difference between real and pretend journeys. Share memories of journeys you and the children have had.
3. Now show the children the empty box and ask them what else you would need to find so that you can retell the story. Help the children to collect the things you need. Accept the children's ideas of food for the journey, what the Little Bear could use for a space helmet.
4. Read the story for them while they act it out. You may have to do this several times so everyone who wants to can have a go.

Further activities and curriculum links:

▶ In the story The Owl Went Too, during circle time ask the children who they would take with them. Why? (PSED, CLL)

▶ What food would you take? Make collage plates of 'Our Favourite Food' to take to the moon. (CD, PD, KUW, CLL)

▶ Send a postcard back from the moon. (PD, CLL, CD).

▶ Find some non-fiction books about space and night. Read them with the children and use them as inspiration for stories, pictures, drama and dance. (CLL, CD, KUW, PD)

And another idea...

▶ On a wet day, put on your wellies and pretend you are moon walking.

▶ Turn your role play area into a rocket, use silver foil, foil camping blankets, black sheeting for the sky, and hang up stars and planets.

Some Key Words
▶ moon
▶ astronaut
▶ rocket
▶ picnic
▶ boots
▶ stars
▶ lift off
▶ space suit
▶ journey
▶ near/far

Hunting for a Bear

Focus: an expedition in miniature

The container: cat litter trays

What you need

- five cat litter trays filled with the following materials to simulate the physical environment the Bear Hunt travelled through
- Tray 1: grass, hay or straw
- Tray 2: water (the river)
- Tray 3: wet compost (oozy mud)
- Tray 4: leaves and twigs (the forest)
- Tray 5: shaving foam (a snow storm)
- a doll's bed
- an upturned box for the cave
- the bear
- some small world people
- a copy of the book 'We're Going On a Bear Hunt' (published by Walker Books)

This lovely story lends itself to lots of tactile experiences. Children love the hunt trail and the onomatopoeic words describing the journey. Make this series of boxes for some experiential small world play.

What you do

1. Put the trays on the table or the floor and cover them with a sheet.
2. Read the story, enjoying the hunt, the journey, the words and making it an exciting read with a climax when the hunters run back to bed.
3. Uncover all the boxes with the stages of the journey and talk about each one, retelling the words that go with each stage – 'swishy, swashy grass,' 'splishy, sploshy water', etc. Let the children feel the materials with their hands as you say the words together.
4. Now use the small world people to play out the Bear Hunt. You could read the story as the children move the people across the line of trays.

Further activities and curriculum links:

▶ Make a collage map of the Bear Hunt, sticking on grass, blue paper for the water, chocolate spread or clay for the mud, leaves and twigs for the forest and white paint and glitter for the snowstorm. (CD, PD, CLL, KUW)

▶ During circle time, discuss with the children how the bear only wanted to be friends with the family but they all ran away – how do you think he felt? The family were frightened – what makes you frightened? (CLL, PSED)

And another idea...

▶ Make an outdoor obstacle course of the Bear Hunt. Encourage children to go under, over and through the obstacles.

▶ Help the children to build their own bear cave using blankets and rugs.

Some Key Words
▶ over
▶ under
▶ through
▶ bear hunt
▶ cave
▶ safe
▶ scared
▶ run
▶ hide
▶ adventure

The Goldilocks Box

Focus: cook up a story

> **The container: a large storage crate**

What you need

- a large storage crate
- a picture book of 'Goldilocks and the Three Bears'
- laminated picture cards of the three bears, their beds, chairs and bowls (for sorting and matching)
- masks/ears/hoods for the bears
- small, medium and large sized bowls and spoons

- ingredients for making biscuits
- mixing bowl, scales, spoons
- a baking tray
- a cooking timer
- aprons
- teddy bear cutters
- ingredients for porridge
- a wig for Goldilocks

I will need

> Young children love this story and are familiar with it from a very young age. It offers lots of opportunities for sizing and cooking and of course, joining in with the chanted questions. Cooking is also a wonderful way to learn about size, shape and the fun of sharing food.

What you do

1. Use the masks, wigs or hats and other props from the box to retell the story. Leave the box where children can use it again in free play.
2. Do some Three Bears cooking – make some graded teddy bear biscuits or porridge. Serve the porridge in graded bowls and eat with the matching spoons.
3. See how many things you can collect that start with 'b'.

Further activities and curriculum links:

▶ Add different things to the porridge: i.e. sugar, jam or the Scottish addition of salt. Allow the children to try each, and make a teddy pictogram showing which one they preferred. (KUW, PSED, PD, MD)

▶ What do bears in other stories like to eat? How about Paddington or Winnie the Pooh. Try honey and marmalade on toast. Which do the children like best? What do they like to have on their toast? Try other favourites such as jam and Marmite. (CLL, KUW, PSED, PD)

▶ The bear in 'Whatever Next?' takes his own picnic to the moon. What do you like to eat? What would you take in your moon picnic? (CLL, PSED, KUW)

And another idea...

▶ Baby Bear's chair was broken. Could we build another one out of large construction bricks, boxes or from wood from the woodwork bench?

▶ Make some new songs about three - such as: **Three Brown Buns, Three Speckled Frogs, Three Little men in a Flying Saucer, Three Green Bottles.**

Some Key Words
▶ big
▶ middle
▶ little
▶ Mother
▶ Father
▶ Baby
▶ porridge
▶ count
▶ choose
▶ best
▶ like

Three Little Pigs

Focus: another story about 3

> **The container: a small tool or hobby box**

What you need

- a small tool box
- the story of 'The Three Little Pigs'
- finger puppets of the three pigs and the wolf
- a builder's tray
- materials to make models of the houses – straw, kindling, balsa or ply wood, Lego bricks (or bricks made from salt dough, baked hard)

- glue, string, card, scissors, etc.
- model pigs, wolf, trees, etc. for the story setting

Children (especially boys) love tool boxes – get several small ones from DIY stores, so more than one group can play. The Three Little Pigs story links well with topics on construction and homes, and could run alongside some 'Bob The Builder' boxes.

What you do

1. Read the story to the children. The children could help by using the puppets.
2. Talk about what our houses are made of. You could go on a local walk and look at building materials used in your area. Take some photos to talk about when you get back. Ask the children why they think houses are not made from straw or sticks.
3. Look at the box and the materials together. Talk about which materials made which house.
4. Now leave the children to work with the materials to make some houses of their own. Offer help if they need it.
5. Watch how they work and add extra materials if they need them.
6. Use the builder's tray to make a small world setting for the story and retell the story using small world animals.

Further activities and curriculum links:

▶ Begin a project on houses – look at houses in other countries and the materials they are made of. (KUW)

▶ Take the children for a local walk to look at the different types of houses – detached, semi detached, terraced, bungalows, flats. (KUW)

▶ Go and look at a local building site (ask first!) (KUW, CLL)

▶ The bear in 'Whatever Next?' takes his own picnic to the moon. What do you like to eat? What would you take in your moon picnic? (CLL, PSED, KUW)

And another idea...

▶ If you are near a canal, go and look at a narrow boat or house boat.
▶ Arrange a visit to a show home or invite a builder to visit your setting to talk about how houses are built.

Some Key Words
▶ straw
▶ brick
▶ wood
▶ house
▶ home
▶ detached
▶ semi
▶ terrace
▶ bungalow
▶ flat

Mr Gumpy's Outing

Focus: **a box or a boat?**

What you need

- ▶ box for boat
- ▶ headbands of the characters (not the children): you need Mr Gumpy and the rabbit, cat, dog, pig, sheep, chickens, calf and goat
- ▶ blue fabric for the river
- ▶ a picnic blanket and picnic food
- ▶ a copy of the book 'Mr Gumpy's Outing' (published by Red Fox).

A big plastic box, or a baby bath is a good thing to use for this activity. You can get boxes cheaply from bargain shops or **DIY** stores. The story is about a boat ride that gets more and more complicated. It's good for sequencing and looking at different characters.

What you do

1. Read the book with the children, using the masks to help with the characters. Invite the children to go on Mr Gumpy's outing. Re-enact the story of the goat kicking, the calf trampling, and all the other animals behaving badly, until finally the boat tips over. Use the blue fabric to make the water.

2. At the end of the story they go home for tea. Perhaps you could have a picnic (or tell the story just before snack time).

3. Talk with the children about what happened in the story, and why the boat tipped over.

4. Talk about picnics, what you eat, where you go, what you need to take.

5. Leave the box where children can play with it in free choice sessions.

Further activities and curriculum links:

▶ Make a story board, so the children can tell the story to each other – use a felt scenery backing and laminated characters with Velcro on the back. (CLL, CD)

▶ Use small world animals to tell the story again. Make a real river outside and use a toy boat. (CLL, CD)

And another idea...

▶ Try putting small world animals in toy boats in the water tray. See how many can fit in before it sinks.

▶ Make boats and a waterway outside with guttering.

Some Key Words
▶ boat
▶ sink
▶ float
▶ tip
▶ water
▶ soaking
▶ picnic
▶ make
▶ journey
▶ behave

Little Bear's Bag

Focus: a night time bag

The container: a large plastic crate

What you need

- a bear shaped back pack or a draw string bag in fur fabric or bear print
- dark drapes to make the cave – clip stars and the moon to the top of the outside of the cave
- Father Bear's glasses (just frames are safer – ask an optician for out of date children's frames)
- a blanket for a pretend bed
- a copy of the book 'Can't You Sleep, Little Bear?' (published by Walker Books)
- lanterns
- torches
- cassette player and blank tapes

I will need

Another story which links with a maths topic on size, or a day and night topic (see Time and Place boxes on page 40). Many children will empathise with the little bear who is afraid of the dark. Exploring scary feelings in safe surroundings is an important part of children's experiences in the Foundation Stage.

What you do

1. With the help and suggestions of the children, make a bears' cave for the story.
2. Get inside the cave and read the story (perhaps by torchlight).
3. Use the props to help the children take part in the story.
4. You will probably need to tell the story several times, so everyone can have a turn!
5. Talk about the sounds of the night, look at fact books, perhaps a video of animals and birds of the night.
6. Leave the cave for:

   -free play

   -other group sessions to talk about the dark

   -a quiet place for children to rest and reflect

Further activities and curriculum links:

▶ Talk to the children about why Little Bear was not able to get to sleep. Let them talk about what frightens them. Who makes them feel better? How can they make their friends feel better when they are sad, scared or worried? (PSED, CLL).

▶ Show the children how to use the DVD inside the cave to re-tell the story. (CLL, KUW).

And another idea...

▶ Make night time pictures with purple, black and yellow paint or pens.
▶ Use torches to make shadows inside your cave. Try making shadow shapes of soft toys, animals, people on the walls.

Some Key Words
▶ torch
▶ lantern
▶ night
▶ dark
▶ big
▶ little
▶ middle
▶ star
▶ moon
▶ scared

Yes We Can!

Focus: Bob and his friends!

The container: a large wheeled box

What you need

- a big, strong box with wheels and a handle
- wooden, plastic or real bricks
- plastic cones to fence off the site
- 'DANGER' sign
- 'STOP/GO' signs to stop traffic (trikes and bikes in the garden)
- a large spirit level
- tape measure and metre stick

- child-sized hard hats
- yellow safety vests
- child's plastic or wooden small role play tool set (or real, child size tools)
- sand, trowels, small buckets
- small tool boxes, clip boards, pens

you could also add:
- toy lorries, trucks, tractors and diggers

I will need

You need a big box for this activity, preferably one with wheels, so children can pull it along as they play. It needs to be strong enough to carry heavy things. The Builders' boxes could be part of a topic on houses, and will go well with the Builders' and Three Pigs' boxes.

What you do

1. This is an outdoor activity. Let the children help you set up the building site and arrange the equipment ready for play.

2. Walk round the site with the children and talk about what happens, how things work, what they are for, and site safety.

3. Stay close to the activity as children begin to use the equipment and toys in role. Use your judgement about whether you need to restrict group size (it will probably need to be adjusted depending on the space and amount of equipment you have).

4. At the end of sessions, encourage the children to talk about what they have been doing. Offer additional resources if they ask for them, and feed back to them what you have seen.

Further activities and curriculum links:

▶ Introduce problems for the children to solve – building a particular size wall, measuring things, lifting/carrying heavy loads, etc. (CLL, MD)

▶ Bob's Maths Workshop box – This box needs careful supervision and clear rules. It contains nails, tacks, small, real hammers, polystyrene blocks, wood blocks, card strips. Show the children how to put the nail in a card tab so they can hold it safely as they hammer into wood or thick polystyrene. (KUW, CD, MD)

And another idea...

▶ Play a video of a real building site. Get books and pictures to help the children with their play.

▶ Use their growing skills and interest to build small constructions (beds, walls, tubs) for the garden.

Some Key Words
▶ build
▶ brick
▶ tools
▶ nails
▶ hammer
▶ calculator
▶ price
▶ deliver
▶ drive
▶ digger

A Letter for You!

Focus: post, deliveries and parcels

The container: a post sack

What you need

- a large post sack which can be hung on a hook when not in use
- a box or packet of forms (ask your local post office)
- old stamps (or make some by sewing lines across sheets of paper with a sewing machine and no cotton)
- date stamp
- small scales to weigh parcels
- 'AIR MAIL' 'FRAGILE' 'DO NOT BEND', etc. – as stickers
- numbered mail sorting trays
- envelopes, some addressed with numbers, to sort in the trays.
- postcards, pens, money
- parcels and packages
- telephone, computer keyboard, clock, calendar, phone book

You can use a character familiar to the children to introduce this theme. Postman Pat is a well loved character, and may tempt even reluctant role players to join in. Putting the activity in a large sack makes it easy for the children to transport to a play space indoors or outside.

What you do

1. Collect some of the items and let the children help you to set up the Post Office.

2. Talk about what postmen and postwomen do. Ask those children who have been in a Post Office what happens there.

3. Tell a Postman Pat story or play a video.

4. If possible, arrange a visit to your local Post Office. Talk about the visit before you go, take some photos of the inside and the outside of the Post Office. You may be able to see a sorting office or the parcel depot.

5. When you get back to your setting, talk about any additions to the Post Bag, and any improvements you need to make to the Post Office. Make a book of the photos and add it to the bag.

Further activities and curriculum links:

▶ Sort the post – matching the numbers. (CLL, MD, PD)

▶ Weigh parcels – which is the heaviest? (CLL, MD, KUW)

▶ Buy stamps (use real money if possible). (CLL, MD)

▶ Provide a post bag and let the post person get on their delivery bike to deliver the post to the other children. (CD, CLL)

And another idea...

▶ Make a corner where children can write letters. Provide a post box and a list of children's names.

▶ Use your outside area as a parcel office – make lots of parcels to shift, carry, deliver, sort.

Some Key Words
▶ letter
▶ stamp
▶ parcel
▶ deliver
▶ pay
▶ sort
▶ post box
▶ money
▶ envelope
▶ postcard

What's in The Box!

Focus: mysteries and surprises

> **The container: a range of different boxes**

What you need

- a range of interesting boxes of different sizes, shapes, patterns, fastenings. A box could be any of the following:
- sent by post in brown paper
- wrapped in bubble wrap
- wound round and round with ribbon
- decorated with bows and labels with a 'This Way Up' sticker
- tiny, in a plastic bag
- hidden in the garden
- hanging from a tree
- locked, with a key to hunt for
- knotted up with string
- delivered to your setting
- very big and light
- very heavy
- noisy
- covered in little holes

The boxes should not be opened immediately, so children can speculate, imagine and guess what might be hidden inside. This arouses much interest, excitement and imagination! Children can admire and touch the contents, who they might belong to and why they have been left.

And the contents could be (some suggestions):

A bunch of keys; a pair of shoes; a snow storm; a tiara; an invitation; a letter; an little album of photos; a dog lead; a fake jewel; a ring; a lost teddy bear; a tiny cup; a very big shirt; a wand; a book in another language, etc.

What you do

1. Put the box in the middle of the circle of children. Tell the children where you found it, or how it arrived in your setting.

2. Now pass the box round, looking carefully at the outside, turning it over, shaking it gently, wondering aloud what might be inside. Let everyone have a turn at guessing what is inside. Encourage them to look for clues on the box and from the feel of it.

3. Now decide who will open the box. You will need to devise some way of choosing – don't always do it yourself! Encourage the child to be very careful so they don't spoil what is inside. Talk them through the process.

4. There may be another layer (tissues, bubble wrap, fabric, cotton wool) before you get to the object. Keep the suspense going!

5. Finally you see what is in the box. Lift it out and hand it round so everyone can feel it in their hands. Now start imagining!

And another idea...

▶ Fill a box with different hats (a baby's bonnet, a football hat, a sun hat, a baseball cap, a policeman's helmet, a fireman's hat, a wedding veil, a builder's hard hat, a chef's hat, a nurse's hat). Who do they belong to?

▶ Visit a local packaging factory to see boxes being made.

Some Key Words
▶ box
▶ surprise
▶ imagine
▶ inside
▶ wrapped
▶ present
▶ gently
▶ shake
▶ favourite
▶ listen

My Box, Your Box

Focus: **personal interest boxes**

The container: **a shoe box**

What you need

- ▶ a small box – an old shoe box is ideal
- ▶ items that the child is interested in (these can come from home as well as your setting)
- ▶ children with special needs (and particularly children whose needs are on the autistic spectrum) often develop special interests in a TV character, a type of toy, an animal

- ▶ The child, or children could decorate the box with relevant pictures, drawings, words, collage materials, etc.

An interest box is a collection of objects that appeals either to a group of children, or the current topic (a bucket of items from the seaside). It could be a collection of natural materials (found on a walk), or a basket of very small containers (a special interest is sometimes called a schema).

What you do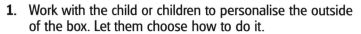

1. Work with the child or children to personalise the outside of the box. Let them choose how to do it.

2. Talk to them about what they want to put in the box. This of course will depend on the interest. You may wish to provide the first few things to give the children a start.

3. Encourage children to bring objects from home to add to their box. Give them a special place to store the box, and let them play with it in free choice time as well as for discussion and focused work. Children with special educational needs (SEN) can play with their own box as a break from more formal activities.

4. Always have some empty boxes handy so other children can make their own personal treasure box.

5. Use the boxes for one-to-one or small group activities – discussion, language development, creative and imaginative play with the objects, pictures and people inside

6. Always ask before using the boxes with other children. They often become very special to the individual, who may become very anxious and protective if their privacy is not respected.

And another idea...

▶ Encourage children with special needs to share their boxes with other members of the group. This allows the child to have some autonomy over an activity which they may not always experience.

Some Key Words
▶ inside
▶ favourite
▶ mine
▶ special
▶ best
▶ choose
▶ decorate
▶ keep
▶ make
▶ share

An Empty Box

Focus: **endless possibilities!**

The container: **big cardboard cartons**

What you need

Very big boxes from:

- washing machines and other white goods
- TVs and computers

- furniture
- school equipment, in fact, any box big enough for one or more children to get inside

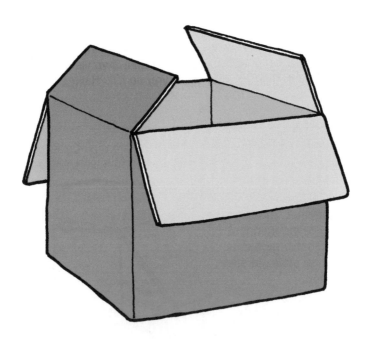

Practitioners constantly endeavour to provide resources which enthuse children and offer good learning opportunities. We also need to protect children's own play, imagination and creativity. One way to encourage child initiated play and learning is to provide simple empty boxes of all sizes.

What you do

1. Leave the box in a space (indoors or out) and GO AWAY – far enough away to stop yourself influencing what happens!

2. Watch what happens. You could take some unobtrusive photos.

3. Children will soon begin to congregate and negotiate on the use of such a wonderful toy.

4. If they ask you, get involved in the activity by providing things they need. They may ask for:
   string, glue, sellotape
   scissors or for you to cut windows or doors
   further card, other boxes, tubes, etc.
   paint, paper, labels, pens, chalk.

5. If they feel relaxed and independent, they may fetch furniture, toys, props and fabrics to extend their play.

6. You may be involved by the children in their discussions or disputes, but try to encourage them to work out their problems themselves. Don't give them solutions or your views, just reflect their own views back to them – ask 'What do you think?', 'How could you do it?', 'Have a think about that.'

And another idea...

▶ Try to provide this sort of big box play regularly. Children will get used to working together, and will become more independent and able to solve problems. Ask your local stores to save boxes for you.

The Little Books Club

There is always something in Little Books to help and inspire you. Packed full of lovely ideas, Little Books meet the need for exciting and practical activities that are fun to do, address the Early Learning Goals and can be followed in most settings. Everyone is a winner!

We publish 5 new Little Books a year. Little Books Club members receive each of these 5 books as soon as they are published for a reduced price. The subscription cost is £37.50 – a one off payment that buys the 5 new books for £7.50 instead of £8.99 each.

In addition to this, Little Books Club Members receive:
- Free postage and packing on anything ordered from the Featherstone catalogue
- A 15% discount voucher upon joining which can be used to buy any number of books from the Featherstone catalogue
- Members price of £7.50 on any additional Little Book purchased
- A regular, free newsletter dealing with club news, special offers and aspects of Early Years curriculum and practice
- All new Little Books on approval - return in good condition within 30 days and we'll refund the cost to your club account

Call 020 7440 2446 or email: littlebooks@acblack.com for an enrolment pack. Or download an application form from our website:
www.acblack.com/featherstone